The Red Virgin

The Brittingham Prize in Poetry

The University of Wisconsin Press Poetry Series
Ronald Wallace, General Editor

Places/Everyone • Jim Daniels
C. K. Williams, Judge, 1985

Talking to Strangers • Patricia Dobler
Maxine Kumin, Judge, 1986

Saving the Young Men of Vienna • David Kirby
Mona Van Duyn, Judge, 1987

Pocket Sundial • Lisa Zeidner
Charles Wright, Judge, 1988

Slow Joy • Stefanie Marlis
Gerald Stern, Judge, 1989

Level Green • Judith Vollmer
Mary Oliver, Judge, 1990

Salt • Renée Ashley
Donald Finkel, Judge, 1991

Sweet Ruin • Tony Hoagland
Donald Justice, Judge, 1992

The Red Virgin: A Poem of Simone Weil • Stephanie Strickland
Lisel Mueller, Judge, 1993

The Red Virgin

A Poem of Simone Weil

Stephanie Strickland

The University of Wisconsin Press

The University of Wisconsin Press
114 North Murray Street
Madison, Wisconsin 53715

3 Henrietta Street
London WC2E 8LU, England

5   4   3   2

Printed in the United States of America

Library of Congress Cataloging-in-Publication Data
Strickland, Stephanie.
The red virgin: a poem of Simone Weil / Stephanie Strickland.
88 p.   cm.—(The Brittingham prize in poetry)
ISBN 0-299-13990-5.   ISBN 0-299-13994-8 (pbk.)
1. Weil, Simone, 1909–1943—Poetry. 2. Women philosophers—
Poetry. 3. Philosophy—Poetry. I. Title. II. Series.
PS3569.T69543R43   1993
811'.54—dc20   93–12949

Grateful acknowledgment is made to the following publications in which these poems, or earlier versions of them, first appeared:

America: "Never but One"

The American Voice: "Comic Progression, 1939–," as "Simone Weil: Comic Progression, 1939–"

Calapooya Collage: "Unconverted: Bede's Sparrow," as "Bede's Sparrow"

5 AM: "Bloom as Blue Grapes"

Iris: "Your Death: What Is Said," as "Starving: What Is Said"

Ironwood: "Airdrill"; "At Home," as "At Home: Simone Will Always Come Back Home"; "Consent"; "Counterweight"; "In the English, the Provençal and Irish poems . . ."; "Gertrude Stein, Paris . . . ," as "Gertrude Stein, from *The Making* . . ."; "Gustave Thibon, *How Simone Weil Appeared to Me/*1–4"; "How You Are Withheld from Me"; "Letters from Mme. Weil . . ."; "Necessity," as "Obedience"; "Still Darning a Sock," as "Young Professor"; "When from the Depth"; "Zealot in a Zoo"

New Virginia Review: "Absent from Dances, 1925," "Agent," "Fig Tree," "Justice," "Revelation"

Prairie Schooner: "Bench-Hand: 'The Famous "Real Life," ' " "Dignity," as "My Dear Albertine"; "Excused for Illness"; "Love Affair, Fourth Century," as "Love Affair: Fourth Century"; "Names / Ugliness," as "Ugliness"; "Soul Learns Everything from Body"; "War Rations Chosen, London, 1943"

Songs for Our Voices: Award-Winning Poetry on the Jewish Experience, edited by Paula Naomi Friedman and published by The Judah L. Magnes Museum, 1993. Berkeley, CA, "Cut at the Root: Simone Weil, 1909–1943," a sequence of twelve poems: "De Beauvoir, from *Memoirs of a Dutiful Daughter,*" as "Simone de Beauvoir, . . ."; "Defilement," as "Everyone Despises"; "How Imperatives Enter the Body"; "Interview with André Weil, 1973," as "BBC Interview . . ."; "Intact"; "Revolution: Simone at 27"; "Jews"; "Quality"; "Unregarded Source"; "Xeres: Take this Cup," as "Take this Cup"; "Xmas Pudding"; "Chronology"

I wish to express my deepest thanks to the Corporation of Yaddo for the time and space they permitted me, and I would like to thank those whose taxes supported this work through a grant awarded by the National Endowment for the Arts.

As for the Red Virgin,

we shall leave it to her to make bombs

for the coming grand social upheaval.

—C. Bouglé, Acting Director
Ecole normale supérieure

We shall send the Red Virgin

as far away as possible

so that we shall never hear of her again.

—C. Bouglé, Director of Career Placement
Ecole normale supérieure

Contents

Note

Simone Weil's actual or paraphrased remarks are given in italics. Document excerpts are credited in the titles of poems where they are used. Thibon's remarks are to be found scattered in his portion of the account *Simone Weil as We Knew Her*, by J. M. Perrin and G. Thibon (London: Routledge & Kegan Paul, 1953, translated from the French by Emma Craufurd). Mme. Weil's letters and Simone de Beauvoir's remarks are quoted in Simone Pétrement's biography, *Simone Weil, A Life* (New York: Pantheon Books, 1976, translated from the French by Raymond Rosenthal). A transcript of André Weil's interview with the BBC appears in *Gateway To God: Simone Weil,* edited by David Raper (Glasgow: William Collins Sons & Co., 1974). Letters to her family, to her pupil, to Albertine Thévenon and to Jean Giraudoux appear in *Simone Weil, Seventy Letters,* translated and arranged by Richard Rees (London: Oxford University Press, 1965). The Gertrude Stein passages are from *The Making of Americans* (New York: Something Else Press, originally published 1925, reissued 1966). Paul West's essay appears in his book, *The Wine of Absurdity: Essays on Literature and Consolation* (University Park: Pennsylvania State University, 1966). I have drawn heavily on Jacques Cabaud, *Simone Weil: A Fellowship in Love* (London: Harvill Press, 1964).

Chronology

1909–28   Simone Weil is born in Paris, 3 February 1909, to an affluent Jewish family. Her brother, André, a mathematical prodigy, is three when she is born. Educated with—and by—her brother, at 16 she enrolls in the *Lycée Henri IV* in an all-male class. In the entrance exams for the *Ecole normale supérieure,* she places first. Simone de Beauvoir is second. Behind them, thirty men.

1928–31   At the *Ecole normale,* she publishes an essay on the nature of work and writes her thesis, *Science and Perception in Descartes.*

1931–32   While teaching in Le Puy, she is an active trade unionist. An episode in which she leads the unemployed to the mayor's office and the city council chamber results in her transfer.

1932–34   After investigating German trade unions and the German Communist Party, she publishes an analysis predicting a Nazi-Soviet non-aggression pact. While teaching at Roanne and Auxerre, she demonstrates against police brutality, armaments manufacture, and miners' unemployment.

1934–35   She begins work as a factory hand. Laid off after four months, she obtains, and loses, two subsequent positions.

1935–36   Teaching in Bourges, she experiences newly severe chronic headaches. In Spain, she offers her services as a soldier to the Anarchist Union's militia, but is injured in an accident.

1937	Visits Switzerland and Italy.
1938	In Holy Week, she goes to the Abbey of Solesmes to hear plain-chant. Introduced to George Herbert's poems by another visitor, she begins to make a practice of reciting Herbert's "Love III."
1939–40	Writes on the origins of Hitlerism. Also drafts and submits to the government a "Memorandum on the Formation of a Front-line Nursing Squad." The Weils flee to unoccupied France.
1941	In Marseilles, she meets Father Perrin, a Dominican monk working to help refugees. At her request, he sends her to Gustave Thibon to work as a field-hand.
1942	Routed through Morocco and New York, she arrives in London, where she works for De Gaulle's Ministry of the Interior.
1943	In April, she is admitted to Middlesex Hospital. She refuses food and refuses treatment for tuberculosis. Transferred to a sanatorium in Ashford, Kent, she dies August 24.

The Red Virgin

In the English, the Provençal and Irish poems,
joy so pure it hurts; in Greek poems, pain so pure
it soothes: the mind becoming relaxed
descends a little, from its greatest
concentration, and spreads out in words;
love does the same, in acts.

This is how she talks, too focal, too close
to the tension in her thought. I would descend
lower still, bring her near me, gossip
about her, paraphrase. If I distort,
I don't abandon.
                Come to her
yourself: we each build our own scaffold.

Absent from Dances, 1925

Black, Byzantine eyes
seize us like falcons.
We are defended, a bit,

by the wire-rims;
by lips, unreasonably
full. Awkward hips, long

tent skirts. Stuffing an inkpot
down the pocket
of her beige one—the stains,

huge, black suns
spreading on
the skirtfront, Simone!

at sixteen
you should have been more lady-
like, less mood, less

burning.
At fourteen,
I thought of dying.

My brother, his exceptional
gifts, brought
my own

inferiority
home to me. I did not mind
the lack of visible

successes . . . what did
grieve me . . . being excluded—Truth
reserved for genius.

Agent

How do you say her?

      Simone. Say Simone.

But she signs
her letters, *Your affectionate
son, Simon—*

      she's divided,
      always going half-way,
      a double agent.

How do you say Weil?

      Not *Vile,* not the German,
      although I would be pleased
      to call her *Miss Because,*

      but as the family said it,
      Vyay, Vey, an oversound
      of woe, of one

      who waits, keeps vigil.
      To us, a *way* away,
      unavailing.

At Home

So, what do you see from these high windows
besides that great white dome and Eiffel's tower?

>*Trees that burn like broomstraw in the wind—*
>*Glare.*
>*Pain when I gaze.*

You who so greatly fear your blindness,
why not turn from the window?
Introduce us, Simone. Who is this?

>*Mime,*
>*my mother, Mime, who fills*
>*this room with photographs.*

>*I am the cherub on the table.*

>*That is Mme. Reinherz,*
>*grandmaman, a pianist; born in Vienna,*
>*family from Galicia. Sometimes*

>*I tease her: nationality suspect.*

>*Grandmother Weil, who lives on rue*
>*de Paradis in the winters.*
>*She is Orthodox, her piety*

>*anomalous, in our world*

>*of standards for thinking.*
>*André and I—*

That boy
with whom you touch heads and laugh?

We had gone begging for candy.
André and I—childish slyness—
told the neighbors

Our parents starve us.

Bench-Hand: "The Famous 'Real Life'"

(To a pupil) *You said in your letter that you were impatient to escape from this unreal life and to find yourself at grips with the material necessities of existence. . . . [B]elieve me that no one could understand better than I your aspiration for a real life, because I share it. But it is precisely the worst cruelty of our time that it makes it very difficult to give precise meaning to the words 'real life'. . . . I have taken a year's leave, in order to do a little work of my own and also to make a little contact with the famous 'real life.'*

Screams of metal—jams—
go unheard in the dinning vibration
down on the floor where Simone's hands
prove a source of anxiety

for co-workers who cover, who "carry"
her, on the power press,
on the shearing-machine with no
guard. Management shifts

her job to tending the furnace,
wrestling huge bobbins into deep
ceramic ovens and before they melt,
dragging them out. She can't

get it down, not the force,
not the rhythm. Once, when work
is close to ruin, someone springs in
for her, lowering the door.

Next week, when a strand of hair
gets caught, and the machine pulls out
a woman's scalp, no one speaks
or jumps to help: Simone,

the new girl, says nothing.
As torn as the others, who flinch
and retract, while straining
to stay attuned, enough to sense

the faintest hairline crack
of error—sudden silence, someone's face
blanching. By afternoon, the woman
is back, *on* the machine;

more than injury, or lock-step,
the famous 'real life' is passivity,
self-hate. Fired, Simone returns
to the foreman at quitting time: *Why?*

A month, standing in rain. Hearing
that the man who hires for Renault
is swayed by the appearance
of women workers—though

she's been to him before, now goes
to her schoolfriend, for make-up,
how to use it. On their milling
machine, cuts the end off her thumb;

metal shavings in her hand become
infected, an abcess;
but she learns to change—re-set—
the cutter blade. She is kept on, past

the trial thirty days. She is proud,
pleased, in a way. . . . What is wrong
is not subordination. Not
the machines: *highly attractive*

and interesting. Not hardship,
or that it is monotonous: encounters
with resistance are, she thinks, the heart
of knowledge. Wrong—to be used,

another's tool—the wholeness
of a task gone: body of it pumped up
and screaming at the workers;
mind of it lost, in cool, isolated

drawing-board rooms of managerial
classes. *The fear—the dread—
of what was to come never ceased
oppressing me, until Saturday afternoon.* . . .

De Beauvoir, from *Memoirs of a Dutiful Daughter*

While preparing to enter the Normale, she was taking the same examinations . . . as I. She intrigued me because of her great reputation for intelligence and her bizarre outfit. . . . A great famine had broken out in China, and I was told that when she heard the news she had wept: these tears compelled my respect much more than her gifts as a philosopher. . . . I managed to get near her one day. I don't know how the conversation got started; she declared in no uncertain tones that only one thing mattered in the world now: the Revolution that would feed all the starving people on the earth. I retorted, no less peremptorily, that the problem was not to make men happy, but to find the reason for their existence.

Bloom as Blue Grapes

Hours of intelligence, hours of labor
bloom as blue grapes—

they, along with sunlight and the soil
beneath this city: no less

in the field than on the altar.
People prefer to believe a dream,

some a dream of their power:
a sense of unlimit

the mind, cut off from the hands'
work, battens on, craves.

Flesh turns to food
for others. We believe this

to be so, *only*
when soreness

in our muscles ripples in rows
we have planted. Or harvest.

Airdrill

Crisis in '32 becomes Depression and Simone
has joined rival Unions in order to unite them
in one Force for revolution, but goes alone

to the industrial region where she speaks
with workingmen about their condition and the need
for solidarity—traveling for hours, each way each week

on her day off from her job at the girls' school
in Le Puy. Visiting a mine, she is allowed to try
the compressed-air drill, a jack-hammer. Never

forgetting it, never recovered, riveted, *one body*
with the machine as if added on, like a supplementary
gear; her mind overridden, overwhelmed by vibration,

holding its head driven at the wall of coal: incessant
rapid acceleration appropriate to it—alien to her,
violently bending to service her body clinging to it.

Counterweight

Activist—
        yet she subscribes to the world
as a perfect work in no need
of assistance;

impatient,
        but enjoining herself to wait
nearly motionless, focusing
all hope

on an event
        which will not occur,
and as hope disappears,
worn down, to wait;

woman
        crippling her own dark
and antic loveliness
conscientiously;

Résistante
        who resigns
from the Free French shortly before death,
though without

illusion
        about them when she left
for London—it wasn't
that some

were thugs, but their intolerance
toward
       those they called *collaborator,*
like Thibon, her friend.

Everybody,
       André says,
considered her an enemy,
because she could see through them very quickly.

Comic Progression, 1939–

1. *Send me. I'll organize a Front Line Corps*
   of Nurses. Men, who would otherwise die from shock
   and loss of blood, will live. Send me.

   Rejected.

2. *Since Nazis are inflamed by prestige, by the mystique*
   of the SS, the persistence of services offered
   at great risk, from great love, in the center
   of our battles, will serve as a symbol, a rallying
   image. I will train the women. Send me.

   Rejected.

3. Morale *is* decisive. Though not better armed,
   the Germans sweep Belgium, leave Paris exposed.
   The French call in old men, Weygand
   as commander. *I want to be*
   in Weygand's shoes, Simone tells her friend.

   She—a Pacifist?

4. June 13, 1940. Overnight on the wall,
   PARIS—OPEN CITY—WILL NOT BE DEFENDED.
   Mme. Weil out strolling with her husband
   and Simone sees the sign, makes them run
   to the Lyons station where there is one
   train only, it full. She insists that her husband
   the doctor is needed, *officially* posted, must
   be allowed. Simone wants off the train—

   Mme. Weil says no.

5. To be used in a dangerous mission—to join
   the Resistance: failure, her own,
   all of France's, shaming her; anger turning
   toward expiation. Obsessed with Arjuna's
   obligation to fight when yet he would not
   kill, in Marseilles she reads the *Gita,*
   begins to learn Sanskrit, to study God's action
   in Asian texts. Since she can't get out,
   in 1941, applying to teach.

   > Rejected. A Vichy decree
   > bars Jews from the professions.

6. Arrested and threatened with the company of prostitutes
   in prison, Simone is overjoyed—not believing
   she should force herself on any person and not having,
   otherwise, any means for meeting women in this line.

   > Conviction overturned:
   > the judge finds her unstable.

7. Coming back, to see Father Perrin—in the convent
   waiting all afternoon, she wants to talk about religion,
   believes there to be an insuperable obstacle
   to her conversion; still, she believes she is a person
   of *implicit faith, on the threshold of the Church.*

   > Rejected. Perrin: ". . . a real illusion
   > on her part. At first, she did not
   > seem to be aware of any problem. The love
   > of Christ seemed to be enough for her. Then,
   > she began to understand the doctrinal
   > depth of Catholicism . . . in all seriousness. . . ."

8. Winter-spring '42, in Marseilles she writes,
   I believe one identical thought is expressed precisely
   with slight differences of modality in
   > *Pherekydes,*
   > *Thales,*

Anaximander,
Plato,
Greek Stoics,
Greek poetry of the great age,
universal folklore,
Upanishads,
Bhagavad Gita,
Chinese Taoist writings,
certain currents of Buddhism,
sacred writings of Egypt,
Christian dogma,
Christian mystics,
some Christian heresies, Cathar,
     Manichaean, and
this thought today requires a modern and Western form
of expression. That is to say, it requires to be expressed
through the only approximately good thing we can call our own,
namely science. This is all the less difficult because
it is itself the origin of science.

    Unread, then. Today rejected. Correctly,
    as heretical; wrongly, as syncretic.

9.   Places on a boat booked. *Am I running away?*
     But the Front Line Corps—would Americans? London?
     Seventeen days in Casablanca waiting to board
     the Portuguese steamer. July in New York
     on Riverside Drive. It is 1942.
     With her Plan she sets out—   The Corps

       rejected, by Maritain, Washington,
       the Free French Committee,
       and the Free French Delegation.

10. A contact! Maurice Schumann, schoolmate, spokesman
     for Gaullists in London. Schumann shows the Plan
     to Commissioner Philip—

       he rejects it.

He thinks he can use her.

11. Departure for London arranged. She arrives—is delayed
     for eighteen days in an internment camp. But *Here I am,*
     she says at last, *ready to sabotage—or, to organize.*

> Actually, Miss Weil,
> your desk is here.
> The committee proposals
> for postwar reconstruction:
> look them over—would you?
> Draw some, yourself.

12. *If you won't send me to sabotage, send me to spy.*
     Send me to some place we need to win at the cost
     of a life. I am here— Send me.

> Rejected.

13. Fearing she fails in something commanded, failing
     to perform through lack of energy, faith, or power
     to persuade, for five months she asks to be sent,
     all the while working as an editor for Philip, generating
     proposals for the Free French; long hours, asleep
     at her desk, after the last train bent to her table:
     essays, reports, on the *meaning* of justice, the new
     Constitution, the colonial problem, the war;
     how inadequate Marxism is; how inadequate
     the doctrine of human personality. She writes about
     uprootedness and human obligation. For five
     months. Renewing her request.

> Commissioner Philip: "Why doesn't she
> concentrate on something concrete,
> for instance trade union problems, instead
> of remaining in generalities."

14. She asks to see a priest.

Consent

André: She ate very little.
                She had gotten into habits where she ate
                very little
                out of habit.
                It had always required my mother
                to see to it
                that she fed herself.

André: At the hospital, TB.
                Degenerated from starvation.
                They prescribed overfeeding.
                She ate every day, from April to August.
                She ate very little.

André: Then this sort of vow not to take
                more than the official rations in France,
                which of course Frenchmen
                never did, and for very good reasons.

André: She became unable to put up
                with more food than she was used to.
                She thought, possibly, all of them would meet
                in Algiers, she and my parents.

Simone: *July 1943. Darlings,*
                Remember me to all.

                Dearest M(ime). You think that I have something to give.
                That is the wrong way to put it.
                But I too have a sort of growing inner certainty
                that there is within me a deposit of pure gold
                which must be handed on.
                Only I become more and more convinced
                . . . there is no one to receive it.

It is indivisible. . . . And as it grows,
it becomes more compact.
I cannot part with it piecemeal.

To receive it calls for an effort.

This does not distress me at all. The mine of gold
is inexhaustible.

Defilement

Ice to water, to steam—a structural
change between hurt
and *affliction:* stain
sunk in, a brand
burned
on: someone marked.

We pass quite close and do not notice.

When people live this
acute state long enough, they become
its accomplice, complicity
impeding all effort
—or wish—
for deliverance; then, established

in affliction, they appear satisfied.

Affliction is monotonous.
Cold
as iron, affliction engenders a sense
of defilement crime
should produce
in a criminal, but does not.

Everyone despises the afflicted

to some extent
and admires the criminal. *Why*
of all things in the world is affliction
given power
—to eat
into souls? To possess them?

Dignity

Dear Albertine (1935)

What working in a factory meant for me personally was as follows. It meant that all the external reasons (which I had previously thought were internal) upon which my sense of personal dignity, my self-respect, was based were radically destroyed within two or three weeks by the daily experience of brutal constraint. And don't imagine that this provoked in me any rebellious reaction. No, on the contrary; it produced the last thing I ever expected of myself—docility.

All one's movements are determined all the time by the work. In this situation, thought shrivels up and withdraws, as flesh flinches from a lancet. One cannot be conscious.

In all this I am speaking of unskilled work of course (and especially the women's work).

My dear Albertine (1935)

But all the same I understand certain things which perhaps you don't, because you are too different. You see, you live so much in the moment— and I love you for it—that you perhaps don't realize what it is to see one's whole life ahead and form a steady and fixed resolve to steer it from beginning to end by one's will and effort in a definite direction. If one is like that—and I am like that, so I can understand it—the worst thing in the world that anyone can do to you is to make you suffer in a way that breaks your vitality, and consequently, your capacity to work.

Excused for Illness

Only days at Renault
make you feel enslaved. You fight
for your consciousness, know

from the beginning you cannot
put off the protection class training
and education give. Wretched

with pleurisy. Your father
funds vacations—your mother herself
always going away, to recover

at watering places. This time Portugal,
wretched, too. You wander off
to a small fishing village, come

on the evening of its patronal
festival. Under the full moon,
women with candles, in slow procession

from hovel to boat, are singing,
you say, *what must be very
ancient hymns of heart-rending sadness.*

Fig Tree

One is Genius Itself—the other Beauty,
a neighbor said, pointing
to André,
then Simone, praising
children to their mother.

Simone says, *a beautiful woman*
looking at the mirror may well believe
the image is herself;
an ugly one knows it is not—

She says, she *knows*
it is not, but she shudders, believing
she is the barren, *the parable*
fig tree: naturally
impotent and cursed for her impotence.

Gertrude Stein, Paris, 1925, from *The Making* . . .

p. 166

Many women have at some time resisting in them. . . . Patient women . . . need to have in them a feeling of themselves inside them to be really resisting to any one who owns them. Attacking women . . . have not it in them to need such a feeling for resisting, resisting is natural to them, it covers up in them the weakness of them. Concentrated women . . . are made up of resisting, concentration with them makes the whole of them makes for them the strength such a feeling as themselves inside them gives to patient ones. . . . Such concentrated women have never in them any such resisting in them, yielding is the whole of such ones of them. This needs very much explaining, this makes a history of every kind of woman. . . .

p. 464

It is a very difficult thing to have courage for something no one is thinking is a serious thing.

p. 634

I am realising some sensitiveness in some who have attacking being in them. Soon I will tell complete histories of each one having sensitive being in them. That will certainly be helping to make a long book interesting.

Gustave Thibon, *How Simone Weil Appeared to Me*

I took her on to please my old friend, Father Perrin.
She wanted work on a farm, and he asked me
could I place her somewhere in the Ardeche—

she wouldn't stay at my home, too comfortable
for her, so put me to the trouble of finding her a hut
sufficiently austere. She picked at our meals;

we quarreled about Nietzsche, about God—sometimes I had
to walk away. That first day, I returned to find her
sitting on a tree-trunk in front of the house, lost

in contemplation of the valley of the Rhône;
gradually, her gaze came back to me. To ordinary sight.
No doubt, she owed her hardness to her racial origin—

she was, indeed, the daughter of that People
whom the prophets sought to unbend—and her passionate anti-
Semitism is the most striking evidence of her descent. Is

there anything *more* Jewish than the urge to examine
and test the great realities? Like Spinoza,
still searching for a sign in the refusal of all signs.

Gustave Thibon, *How Simone Weil Appeared to Me/2*

Her magnificent eyes alone
triumphed in that shipwreck of beauty.

Green immaturity: a terrible self-will at the heart
of the self-stripping; a temptation
to verify all from within.

And the way she mounted guard around her emptiness—

I found her unshakable; I never found her
touchy. Unyielding
green fruit.

A poor judge of people, leveling up.

Invincible reserve.

Gustave Thibon, *How Simone Weil*
Appeared to Me/3

Kisses and embraces disgusted her.
I never saw her cry.
She loved tobacco.
Of all the things belonging

to material life, tobacco
was the only one
she was almost certain
to accept. *This smoke*

has been transformed into pages
covered with writing
in my copybooks, she said.
She was counting out one time

the money she had earned
harvesting grapes. I told her
I had no illusions about
the destination

of this sum, whereupon
she replied with disarming
spontaneity, *But*
I shall certainly also buy a few books.

Gustave Thibon, *How Simone Weil Appeared to Me*/4

We are *all*
bargaining with heaven—
Simone Weil's whip

calls us back to order.
The only non-heresy is silence.
Silence,

itself, a kind
of treason. She said, *Truth
is on the side of death,*

and it may be so,
but still, it is
too hard for me, that saying.

Gustave Thibon, *How Simone Weil Appeared to Me*/5

I can still hear Simone's voice in the deserted
streets of Marseilles as she accompanied
me to my hotel in the small hours. She was

commenting on the Gospel. Words issued
from her mouth as a tree yields its fruit.
Her words did not so much translate the truth

as pour it into me, whole and unadulterated.
I felt as if I were being transported
beyond space and time, so that I virtually fed

upon light. The systematic side of her work,
so weak and flat, intelligence in flashes
that can't be strung together. Not pearls.

How Imperatives Enter the Body

From a bed in Middlesex Hospital, concealing
her address, Simone is writing
to her mother . . . *my intelligence is praised*

as fools' foolishness is mocked, to evade
the question, Is what I speak the truth?
She asks to see a priest, who is "annoyed"

by her thought: it will not "grasp . . . itself
satisfactorily, and . . . [will] not accept fixed
starting points. . . ." It seems to him,

"too 'feminine' . . . too 'Judaic'. . . ." Her refusal
of treatment offends Dr. Bennett, who rules
her bed be given up, and she taken

to Kent, where they do not want her.
"We deal with industrial patients here
and feel she will not settle down with us."

How You Are Withheld from Me

Diffidence? Both of us. You raised
on some banner: the cerebral, intransigeant
fragments of your life—

your papers not published, not
together; untranslated, out-of-print.
That the work

is copybook, letter
and draft, hurried entry of some scrap
—and magisterial *essais*.

Coming to me
soured, brought by the distaste
you cause some man or woman; no one

saw what you were doing, not even
you, although you knew
the price you paid. You say,

don't cavil at the mystics
for using words of love: they
are theirs, by right. All

others only borrow. Joy
is your secret, your power to keep
a secret, to keep it implanted,

growing: only closed
lips retain the name of God—how
you are withheld, from me.

Intact

Simone, laying her life in Perrin's hands, has yet
escaped him, has refused the conclusion
of their intimate conversation,

but he has her in his head, safe: no one else
can defame, since she never
confided to paper, but only to him

what had been, till then, intact,
inviolable.
And he, from high-mindedness, will keep it.

Beyond the migraine a music, heard
at Solesmes. Pain
is not gone, but the bondage of pain

is gone. *Fear,* she says,
even a passing one,
sways, or tautens, the mind.

Interview with André Weil, 1973

The BBC: This is something of a Jewish trait, one might say, this deep respect for learning and education?

AW: You might call it that. Actually (my mother's) father, who was by trade a merchant, was a very well-read man who knew Hebrew very well, and in the old days I have seen books of Hebrew poetry written by him.

BBC: But there was no specific practice of Judaism in the family?

AW: No, I even remember that during the war someone told me I was Jewish and I just didn't know what that meant. This is something that could not happen in the modern world, I'm pretty sure.

BBC: I fear not. . . . Given that in the family there was no sort of religious observance, when did you first become aware of your sister's interest in this side of life?

AW: This is . . . not as simple as it appears in the standard biographies. Before she became a student of Alain, she was exposed to a woman who was not directly her teacher but was a teacher in the same lycée, a Jewish woman converted to Catholicism. Apparently she made a strong effort to interest my sister in Catholicism, to the extent that my parents were worried whether she might not get converted.

BBC: They would have disliked it?

AW: At that time they would have disliked it entirely. Being baptized was the most unpleasant thing that could happen to a person in a family with a Jewish background.

Jews

Them, she said,
that people held together
by a terrible violence,

by massacres
they carried out—
those, inflicted on them.

A people
non-assimilable, not
assimilating: so

she indicts *them,*
pushing *her* food away,
blocking *her* baptism.

Justice

As justice is to disregard your strength in an unequal
　　　　relationship and to treat the other
　　　　in every detail, even intonation, posture, exactly

as an equal:
　　　　so God

all-powerful, does not exert power; God waits like a beggar
　　　　for us, made equal, Might drawn
　　　　back

that the world
　　　　be—

As justice: so God, secretly
　　　　present, an opening in us that can move, consent, bond us
　　　　forever,

but not
　　　　appearing—appearing absent; except
　　　　for how a thing can be beautiful, constrained

to its nature, how that
　　　　snares us.

Learning the Lyre

What does it mean to survey
our civilization?

            To understand
how it is that man has become the slave

of his own creations, through what fissure
unconsciousness invades methodical

action. An escape, back to primitive
life, is a lazy solution;

the original Pact—mind
and world—must be re-struck.

That the task
is impossible is no reason not

to undertake it. We are all
like Socrates,

awaiting death in prison,
learning the lyre.

Letters from Mme. Weil
to Mlle. Chaintreuil, André's Tutor

June 1914

This is the kind of little girl that I have come across many times, the kind that leads me to like and esteem boys much more! The levity, the lack of forthrightness, all these little posturings and grimaces in the eyes of the world. . . . I shall always prefer the good little boys, boisterous and sincere, as I see them coming out of the Lycée Montaigne. And I do my best to encourage in Simone not the simpering graces of a little girl but the forthrightness of a boy, even if this must at times seem rude.

June 1915

She is going through a period of irritability and caprices that I can't understand, since nothing in her physical condition explains it. She is indomitable, impossible to control. . . . She stands up to us with an aplomb and assurance that are by now rather comic . . . but that, if continued, will be distressing. . . . I have certainly spoiled her too much, and even now, when she is good, I cannot help but fondle and kiss her much more than I should. And my husband behaves just as I do, because this Simonette is a real woman and is marvelously capable of using her charm when it pleases her to do so.

Love Affair, Fourth Century

Prodigies of asceticism, athletes, champions:
every form of it, entire lives in Syria chained to a pillar;
in Cappadocia liturgical rounds of song
and labor. Is sex debasing?

When the harlot Pelagia rode naked through Antioch,
the clergy hid their faces; but Abba Nilus,
a Father from the Desert, gazed
long and intently at her. Then turning to the rest
he said, *Did not the sight of her great
beauty delight you? Verily, it
greatly delighted me.*

This tradition reaching us through Cassian. The wisdom
of these passionate Fathers consisting in
practical advice. No doctrine,
only instance; no Master,
no system.
Only the body
working. And experience, a lifetime
re-directing: this was what they meant
by prayer. It never ceased. It was a great struggle
to one's last breath. Is sex
debasing?

When Evagrius first came to Scetis he made the mistake
of lecturing these Brethren. They let him
finish. Then one said, *We know,
Father, that if you
had stayed
in Alexandria, you would have been a great bishop.*

To stay—in the cell. To understand the body as a connection:
advice was about where to sleep, what to eat; how to deal
with demons, with passion. *Speak*

a word, Father. Asked over and over. Others
of them; them of each other. And the word
sought was not counsel—
not exposition, nor
dialogue,
nor discussion, but a lifegiving
word spoken once in a relation. Is sex
debasing? It would be
knowledge.

Wary of books, refusing to judge, they led lives of solitude
in stone huts, reed mat for a bed, a sheepskin, a vessel
for water, sometimes oil. *One hour's sleep
is enough for a monk, if he is a fighter.*
One dry meal.

*Be solitary, silent, at peace. If we push ourselves beyond measure
we will break,* Antony said. Antony the Great, unlettered
hermit, said *My life is with my brother,* and returned
to the city, to nurse those with plague
and once, to combat heresy.

Their Sayings cried on a great blank of silence. Spoke only
if before them someone stood. To face
inner conflict without inner lying. To be reticent,
discreet. Simple. They did not trust violence
to instruct them. They did not
trust words: that these two
are not
opposite, *my life is with my brother,
I alone and God are here.*

Is sex debasing? It's hard to bring up in language that says
fuck, to mean exploit. Evagrius, who fled
from a love affair in Constantinople to the care

of Melania, Roman widow, founder of a convent
on the Mountain of Olives; Evagrius
who left her; Evagrius who said, *Restrain yourself*
from affection towards many people, for fear
lest your spirit be
distracted— Evagrius, or Antony,
or Nilus,

or *Simone,* their discovery
about ruin, intellect, passionate God: it's set up
and upset. Sex is
debasing—they are not wrong
about this—is demonic, prodigious, always,
only,
if, for instance, if women
are subordinate.

The Desert left
nothing
to leave: no teaching, no Rule—a mass
of traveler's tales.

Mathematics: Galois

> Evariste Galois,
>   mathematical theorist, 1811–1832
> S. Galois, name taken by S. Weil,
>   writing in *Révolution prolétarienne*

You write of him
as exemplary and stunning,
how he oriented to a mysterious

contradiction—well, I'm tired
of contradiction, tired of riddling,
Simone. No wonder

you wanted to be free
from compulsion: your own,
almost intolerable. Still,

Galois did orient toward
the inconceivable—he, a boy
dead in a duel. And you say

until it's done, good only seems
impossible. Then, when it was,
just see what he had: a field

of roots, of prime
power and identity—in groups,
kernels of a new realm.

My *Not* Burns

What burns in hell?
Divines, doctors, say self-will.
But I say *not*.

If I am not
fire, fire consumes me.
My *not* burns me.

Names / Ugliness

... to make her seem less of a right-minded monster, I fastened avidly on the details of her womanhood. ... The photographs mutely record the decline from her second year, when she was chubby-cheeked with curly black hair the color of her almond-shaped eyes—a pensive, cute doll—to thirty-four, when she starved herself to death in order to share the sufferings of the French. Her face in 1936 is handsome, firm, full-mouthed and rather appealing ... [b]ut five years later she has ... become the headmistress type, owl-eyed through excessive perusal, her expression an odd blend of hennish timidity and impatient pity. And there is a general look of—well: dryness. A sad little gallery of snaps indeed.   —Paul West

They don't know love when they see it.
They think ugliness unfits her for it,
or nicotined fingers, grating voice,
that low monotonous tone, never known
to concede. Love doesn't fail,

either. Love loves what there is:
a bare cupboard—and hunger; though
it be treason, herself, by herself,
France, at her nadir—France still persecuting
what still falls beneath her: Vichy,

shaving the heads of Vietnamese;
an intact elite, the professionals
of language, humiliating
vagrants, women, workers. Love riven
by the cry, *Why am I being hurt?*

but as rain must rain, love must identify
with what is there, with pain, then,

and joy. Love never fails. They don't know
love, when they see it. They call it
names: exigent, frail, audacious in desire—

More alone, even, than she knew.

Necessity

If the sea should alter
the long movement of its waves
to spare a boat,

it would not be beautiful;
but being, at every point, obedient
to infinitesimal pressure of wind, water, light,

being nothing but
obedient, it moves us. We are moved
to venture

on it, not
because the sea will part
for us—

Never but One

manner to serve
a being: give it

food and the movement
it needs. How to love

is in us, imperious
as hunger. We are maintained

by internal coherence,
we get harder

and harder, until under
pressure severe enough

we melt: our fluidity cannot
be made immobile—except

by equilibrium,
running in layers then,

until we rest.
Not needing to ask

how to love: asking only,
what direction.

Numberbody

The world stained to the bone raven blue
with mathematics as an embryo

is stained clear through with amniotic
fluid. Number does not give things

a form. It gives them a body
and makes them understandable—the way

a gnomon makes understandable
eddying of shadow: a sun-dial's witness.

Walk around. Experience
successive appearances produced by the Sun.

By this operation only will you know
what is real: Invariant: the field

that governs the carnations. Deep stain
—if we feel it—reminds us

of amniotic fluid. We are all
obedient: constrained. Necessarily.

But some—Simone—
are consciously obedient,

feeling the absence
like a phantom heart or limb.

On the Wireless

To Jean Giraudoux, Minister of Propaganda in 1939

. . . I would wish you always to speak the truth, even on the wireless.

Did not France acquire Annam by conquest?

We have killed their culture; we forbid them access to the manuscripts of their language; we have imposed upon a small section of them our own culture, which has no roots among them and can do them no good.

I shall never forget hearing an agricultural expert of the Colonial Ministry frigidly explain that people are right to hit the coolies on the plantations because they are so weak from overwork and privation that any other form of punishment would be more cruel.

Past Centuries

To refuse to enter, when you are on the threshold—

but Father—so many
things outside the Church, the whole
immense vista of past centuries
except the last twenty;
everything not white, everything in secular
life, the stunning heresies.

To refuse to bind yourself—

But Father, only in ecstasy, only in division
will the human mind not run away but stay
truthful, in what's painful.

Quality

Men, retaining semen, thereby lay up
superior energy women lack.

Inferiority in genius
—and aspects of sainthood—proceeds

from lack: an ancient indictment
in the Sanskrit. And the Greek.

Semen in a woman? Blue eyes
in a black child. It's our

responsibility, for making her
believe, making her come

to the point where she wants
that—impossibility. Her mother,

of course, made her want it,
first. Simone's mother withdrew

her breast, she herself being
hurt; Simone's mother taught

her daughter to respect
genius, in semen—with certain

awkwardness, Simone has given
back, in every word

of her thought, milk,
and calling it

equivalent, thirst
for milk.

Revelation

She wants. She keeps on wanting and turning
      away and turning and turning until
      she has come back;

she wants to be baptized,
      to be an adherent of Christ in his Church,
      but cannot, can not, because

the Beast, that snarling Crowd-Beast
      in *Revelation,* in Plato, Babylon, none other than
      the Church;

not its faith, the Saints, individual Catholics,
      not liturgy, hymns
      or ceremonies—the record

is Bestial: sanctioned
      genocide in the Old Testament,
      Inquisition;

because the Beast forced and aims to force,
      the Beast reduces
      each luminous proposition,

those she believes
      and understands and would
      contemplate, at greater loving length than almost

anyone, that are for her Icons, reduced
      to the model of statement one undertakes to prove;
      because on pain

of Anathema, non-entry, the Beast
      will force her to state herself, falsely;
      to tie her tongue, mangling its integrity, she who is ready

to give it
        away, her whole mouth as it were
        to devote, but only her own, not some

counterfeit. She knows she is
        destined for disappearance—into ultimate
        Presence, or probable

absence; still,
        this matters,
        this

is a soul.

Revolution: Simone at 27

In Spain on the banks of the Ebro
as Durruti attacks Saragossa,
Simone speaks to peasants

and finds their feeling—sharp
inferiority—exacerbated
by the Revolution: militiamen

tyrannize an unarmed
population; she writes down
her own fear,

also, her lack of it: *how intensely*
everything around me
exists. War without prisoners—

lying on her back, rifle aimed
at the planes. Then she trips
into boiling oil buried in

a cooking pit: too scalded
to move. Silent, for weeks.
Bare, unconnected,

they come then, field-hospital accounts
of massacre, murder,
expeditions to kill Fascists

—*an elastic term,*
as she writes to Bernanos, *used*
for captured children shot.

By the fall of '36, the people's war
is over. She remembers Lenin
demanding a state

in which there would be neither
Army nor police nor a bureaucracy
distinct from the people;

but what emerged, after long civil war,
was a machine. The heaviest ever
laid on that people.

Soul Learns Everything from Body

The bird forgets,
                    but the trap does not. Cassandran,
her harsh voice worrying, probing: *If any*
human being show need of any other, a little
or a lot, why does the latter run away?
I have much experience, on one side or the other.

Everything from the body:
                              a boy
running down the field can *read* so well, his hands
are unimpeded, have already caught the pass;
reached out before
                    he saw. Finally,
not to *read* at all: hands alone
fly up, whole body shaping the air, weaned, immediate.

The soul learns turning,
inclination,
fatigue:
to be worn down.

The body,
unastonished by reduction; it feels
what can be shown:
                    that there exist remarkable
leafless trees of blossom,
                              tiny
back and forth of almond, long, touched, wands of pink
that shudder down their whole length and are blown to the pavement

almost at once—

Still Darning a Sock

Simone brushed aside Albertine Thévenon,
wife of the trade union leader, who answered her door
still darning a sock.

Frowning, the young professor pushed past her
to the back room where Thévenon,
the leader— But in England,

no longer a professor, when she looks at her landlady
standing at the iron, outside it is dark,
blacked out, a notion

of the soul
washed through with woman's work. *Mrs. Francis,*
promise me you won't work so hard—

"Oh and you Miss, that cough. You know
you go with no rest.
Take some tea now, with us."

Mrs. Francis threw roses
into the grave tied with tricolor ribbon. It had been a long ride
on the train—and back to London, working late

at her job
and in the evening, lessons with two boys,
the char work of the house.

There Comes

If you do not fight it—if you look, just
look, steadily,
upon it,

there comes
a moment when you cannot do it,
if it is evil;

if good, a moment
when you cannot
not.

Unconverted: Bede's Sparrow

What if Bede's sparrow for that instant in flight
through the mead hall entering one open end
in the dead of winter found no aisle of calm,

no shelter from storm, but gauntlet fire, the clash
of spear-clang, feasting chieftains? Trapped inside
a pit of roof-beams flying high near the ridgepole,

what if it were glad for light at the end, for clarity
and open air, whether this be full of swirling mist,
ice-like rain, or a blind snow of pine-poles and dark,

floating forests, for it is flying, glad of great
openness, whether it soar the night stung to kindled
points, or is hung in a bell of day's blue, receding light,

or, is nailed to the moon, to a shaft of pure iron,
pulling the sea to vast swells, leaf-bone white.

Unregarded Source

To give up greatness—

For our conception of greatness is the very one which has inspired
Hitler's life.

To have a filial feeling

for your country, but no impulse to compel a worship you cannot
command, but that comes to you, *gratis*, because you are "a citizen"
of that land, that Rome, that Reich—

To shift

from a national wargod to a God of nooks and crannies, a God merely
good, God-of-slaves, -of-the sick. What does it mean—not
to react to, but to resist, Hitler?

To proclaim

a blind woman in a field of lavender, a mystery, initiatory sect
of Egypt, Thrace: *the truth,* Simone says, *has an unregarded*
source . . . unheard story: the truth, taken captive—

What is filial feeling?

In '42, in London, in conversation with Maurice Schumann,
her friend, her schoolmate, fellow Jew, fellow Catholic, Simone
says she is troubled, by parts of the Old Testament,

by Saul and the Amalekites. By the order given there, by
God, for genocide. They had not heard of the concentration
camps, yet, Schumann said.

How can we

condemn a holocaust, today, Simone asks—using that word, that word, later, to Schumann, seeming like a premonition—*if we do not*

　　　condemn all holocausts in the past?

Vertigo / Walk on Water

The generous have overcome their anger,
the zealous have overcome their fear,

those who love have overcome their passion—
charity is horror, overcome. To triumph over

fearsome forces, interpose an obstacle: a rudder
or a bit. Don't wish for anything, neither to control

nor, to submit. You are one who sails a boat. Enormous
masses of wave and wind contend. To balance them,

you. And your tiller. The difference between
sailors is: some understand

the laws that compel them. You can tell
by watching, while they keep their footing, which.

War Rations Chosen, London, 1943

You won't eat. Not more
than the prisoners in France—
Tell the truth, you take less.

To eat the *whole*
ration, yes, a gesture, a symbol
of connection, but you don't;

you divide grams to crumbs,
then refuse them. Hunger interrupts
your task of honoring oaths

you swore to yourself
in disgust: layers of thinking
you shift as often as wind

shifts. Don't confess—not again.
When you were a girl, running,
remember blood, how frightening

to come between your legs?
You starved it away.
How frightening to come, for life,

and not overflow, not empty. Not drain.
Stifled so long, caught in the tree
so long, turned to a tree,

in winter shaking. You, who would be
Apollo, are Daphne, tearless,
harsh. Weeping your skin, with galls

and scale that blisters, one hand against
your mouth. Let it fall, let it pull
the arm down which shields

your breasts. Can you bear this?
Bear them open? As you look
through a broken world, you squint.

Your lenses get thicker. Your angle
of vision sharpens with the sharp,
angling pain in your head.

You have done what you could,
and—it is nothing.
Honor your resistance.

Your Death: What Is Said

The *Kent Messenger* on Friday 3 September, 1943,
reported an inquest at Ashford on Professor Simone A. Weil,
34, late of the University of Paris (*sic*). A woman doctor,
the senior medical officer at Grosvenor Sanatorium, said:

> "I tried to persuade Professor Weil to take some food
> and she said she would try. She did not
> eat, however, and gave as a reason
> the thought of her people in France starving."

The Coroner recorded suicide by starvation
"whilst the balance of her mind was disturbed."

Equilibrium?

The dove

when in free flight it beats the air and feels
that resistance might believe
it would fly even better
in the void—
        You say,
                the soul feels
hindered by its personality, desires it dissolved—
Imperiously wished. Like some flashpoint. Pouf!
through the trap-door.
A hermit wandering in the desert
found the Earthly Paradise. Figs as proof,
he went back to bring the brothers.
They persuaded him so gently,
no Macarius, no.

But you had no others,
no fellowship of Fathers.

Did you judge your death to be a more effective
witness than your life? If so,
you were correct
about us, we leap upon it to hold
against your work. By this
resistance, brought to keep them both

—your thought, your death—

in the mind, polar. There are days when I can see
one through the prism of the other.
The morning, before I went to work,
when my mother choked to death, my mother
who was starving herself,
they slid together.

Some part of me heard "dead" at once,
hissing forward, sucked
into the flesh, but the rest, I lag—
overshoot, begin a process,
false steps varying,
oscillating even, around
a wound I knew I had
received—

"Monster," is said. "Martyr." "Despair."

The words won't make it simple. Death rises
quite as you implied,
not only in the middle of a life,
but at the center.

Zealot in a Zoo

The body is not the soul's opponent:

a soul is injured by the structure of its city,
by mob, by solidarity—by keep
of that Beast: party, program, coerced mode;

the opponent of the soul

is the soul's own words, made to serve,
made-to-measure, to grasp all things
by its grammar.

There are only two services

words offer the afflicted,
the first, to speak of good: good that cannot
be abused;
                then, to speak the numbness
of their affliction, the specific, raw
frantic thing in them—

A tree is rooted in the sky

suspended there
by crystal cannulae, long, clear cables which contain
the falling light. If these are broken

or shrouded, the tree dies.

But if light
                    soar down them, the tree lives, it lives
its body and pushing, sends out roots to bring air into the earth.

Xeres: Take this Cup

It is said, she would allow one
of the nurses to wet her lips
with sherry, that her teeth

clenched when she spoke—
Finally the doctor gave in,
and the order to feed her

by force was rescinded.
In a field not far from
the coroner's court,

workmen prepared
a pauper grave;
for years

unmarked, save
by its Plot
Number.

Xmas Pudding

As she dies of lung infection
unable to rally—refusing nutrition—
she writes on the last page

of her last notebook, *Easter eggs,*
Christmas pudding. She retells
the Irish story, *strawberry jam,*

in which the sister of a youth
who has been executed returns home
and in an upsurge, to throw off

the effect of the death, gorges
herself. The rest of her life,
nausea caused by grief. . . . Attitude

toward food—only real distress
affects it, says Simone. For her,
the filter, the test of what is real,

is flesh—and from this alliance comes
the meaning of meals, on solemn
occasions, or between two

friends, or going out drinking. Last
line, last page: *the most important*
part of teaching = to teach the meaning

of *to know* (*in a scientific*
sense). For, as she says, the trouble
with wishes is, they are granted.

Bearing my scrutiny
first. My adoration. And then
to withdraw . . .

she said of God.
It was also true of André.
True of us all.

She said,

when from the depth
of our being,
we need, we seek a sound

which does mean
something: when we cry out
for an answer,

and it is not granted, then,
we touch the silence
of God—

Some begin to talk,
to themselves, as do the mad;
some give

their hearts to silence.